LOOKING AT LIGHT

BY KAREN A. FRENKEL

TABLE OF CONTENTS

Pictures To Think About	i
Words To Think About	iii
Introduction	2
Chapter 1 What Is Light?	4
Chapter 2 Mirrors and Lenses	12
Chapter 3 Color, Light, and Energy	20
Conclusion	28
Glossary	31
Index	32

Pictures To Think About

Looking at Light

Words To Think About

Characteristics
- clear object
- bends light
- ?

Forms
- raindrop
- crystal
- ?

prism
What do you think the word **prism** means?

concave
What do you think the word **concave** means?

Latin: cum (with)

Latin: cavus (hollow)

Read for More Clues

concave, page 14
prism, page 23
trough, page 7

trough

What do you think the word **trough** means in this book?

Meaning 1
the lowest part of a light wave
(noun)

Meaning 2
a long, narrow container for feeding animals
(noun)

Meaning 3
a shallow, open ditch
(noun)

INTRODUCTION

Could we see without light? Could we live without light? The answer to both questions is no. We could not see without light. We could not live without it, either.

In this book, you will learn about light. You will see what happens when we block light. You will see how light can bend and bounce, too.

◀ Sometimes we see light as it shines off a glass surface.

▲ Most living things need light.

How does light work? How fast is light? Why do mirrors **reflect** (rih-FLEKT), or bounce, light? How do eyeglasses help us see? Why do we see colors? Read on to find out.

Get ready to learn about light!

▼ This light is coming through windows at St. Peter's Basilica in Rome, Italy.

CHAPTER 1
WHAT IS LIGHT?

Light lets us see. During the day, light comes from the sun. When the sky is clear, sunlight is strong. The world looks bright and colorful. On rainy days, light is weaker. Colors seem dull. At night, there is no sunlight. We have to make light to see.

How do you feel when you stand in the sun? You feel warm, right? That is because light gives off heat. Heat is energy. Light is a source of energy.

Light always travels in rays, or beams. The rays fan out from the sun like spokes on a wheel.

◀ Shadows are shortest at noon because the sun's rays strike from directly overhead.

SHADOWS

A shadow appears when something blocks light. Sometimes your shadow is long. Other times, your shadow is short. Why is that?

In the morning, the sun is low. You make a long shadow. That is because you block a lot of light. Sometimes the sun is directly above you. You do not block as much light then. Your shadow is as short as possible. It falls under you, by your feet.

◀ Your shadow is shortest at noon.

▼ Your shadow is longest in the early morning or late afternoon.

CHAPTER 1

Hold a stick close to the ground. The stick's shadow has sharp edges. Now raise the stick higher. The edges of the shadow become fuzzy. The higher the stick, the more light rays spread into the shadow. Other rays hit the edges of the stick. Then the rays spread out, or **diffract** (dih-FRAKT). The rays blur the edges of the shadow.

The fuzzy edges prove that light rays are like waves. If light traveled in straight lines, shadows would always have sharp edges. Some light rays would be totally blocked. Other light rays would pass by without diffracting. Only a wave can diffract.

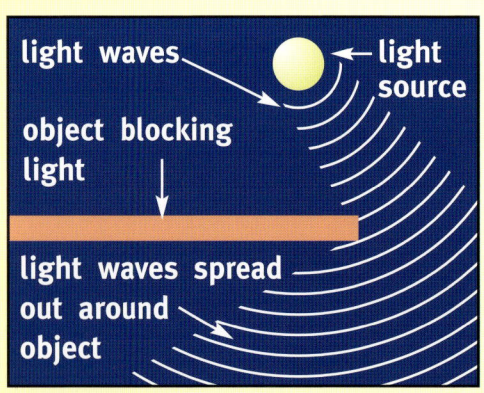

▲ Light spreads into the shadow. This shows that light is like a wave.

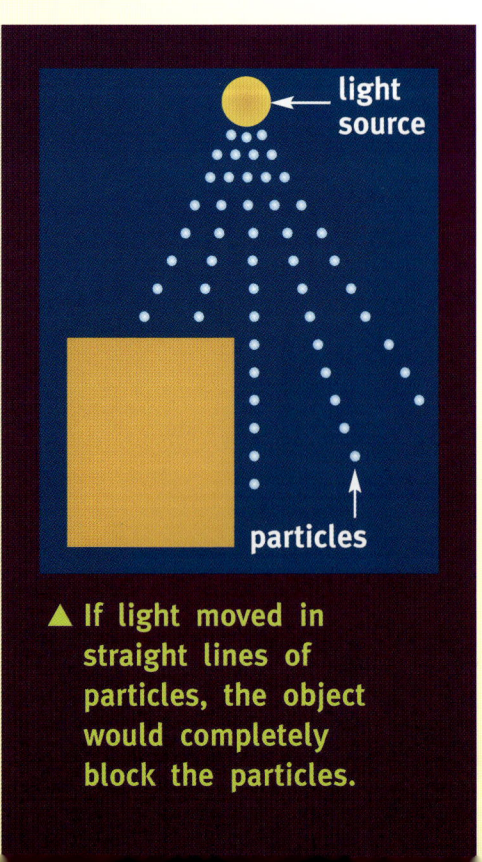

▲ If light moved in straight lines of particles, the object would completely block the particles.

WAVES

Light rays act like water waves. Think of a cork floating in the ocean. The cork moves as it floats. The cork moves because the waves give energy to the cork. Now think of a row of floating corks. A wave gives energy to the first cork, and then to the next cork, and so on.

The high part of a wave is the **crest**. The low part is the **trough** (TROFF). The distance from crest to crest is the **wavelength** (WAYV-lengkth). The closer the crests are, the shorter the wavelength. The shorter the wavelength, the faster the wave moves.

▲ A cork floating on a wave gets energy from the wave.

PICTURE IT
Draw a picture of an object in the sun. Tell a partner why the shadow is long or short and why the edges of the shadow are sharp or fuzzy.

CHAPTER 1

HANDS-ON EXPERIMENT
Interference and Diffraction

Water waves are similar to light waves in several ways. Light waves can combine with each other and so can water waves. When they do, they interfere with each other. You can see for yourself.

- Stack two sets of books so that they are the same height.
- Place white paper on top of the books.
- Get a glass baking dish.
- Rest the dish on top of the paper.
- Pour about 1 inch (2.5 centimeters) of water into the dish.
- Turn out the lights.
- Hold a flashlight about 2 feet (0.6 meters) above the dish.
- Use an eyedropper to drip water into the dish.

You have just created a ripple tank! Look through the side of the dish at the paper and observe the waves that the drops create. The waves begin as half-circles and get straighter toward the edges of the dish. Waves in water spread around objects, or diffract, just as light waves do.

▲ A drop of water creates waves that travel from one end of the dish to the other.

WHAT IS LIGHT?

THE SPEED OF LIGHT

Light has a very short wavelength. That means light travels very fast. Turn on a lamp. The light fills the room instantly. That is because light travels so quickly.

Light can pass through things. When light passes through something, it slows down. The speed of light depends on what it passes through. If light enters something in a straight line, it keeps going in the same straight line. If light enters at a slant, or angle, the ray of light bends.

Math Matters

The speed of light is 186,000 miles (299,338 kilometers) a second. If you could travel that fast, you would circle the globe seven times in one second.

▲ The ray of light bends, or **refracts** (rih-FRAKTS), as it enters this block. It refracts again, in the opposite direction, as it leaves.

CHAPTER 1

Put a straw in a glass of water. The straw appears to be broken. Why? It is because light is passing through different things. Light at the top passes through air and glass. Light at the bottom passes through water and glass. Light travels more slowly through water. The straw looks broken.

▲ Diamonds are bright and shiny because light enters fast and refracts.

▶ The straw appears to be broken at the surface of the water.

Math Matters

The sun is 93,000,000 miles (149,688,992 kilometers) from Earth. How long does light take to reach us? It takes about 8 minutes and 18 seconds for light from the sun to reach Earth.

WHAT IS LIGHT?

MIRAGES

Sometimes light bends in the air. A change in temperature can bend light. When light travels through hot or cold air, it bends. The bending light makes an image. The image is called a mirage (muh-RAHJ). A mirage can look like water.

▲ On a hot summer day, you might think you see a puddle on the road ahead. It is really a mirage.

CHAPTER 2
MIRRORS AND LENSES

Most light we see is reflected. *Reflected* means "bounced off something." Light reflects the most when it hits smooth, shiny things. Mirrors are the best thing for reflecting light.

Look in the mirror. You will see your own image, or reflection. Wave at your image with your right hand. Your image waves back with its left hand. Hold up a card with your name on it. Your name is backward in the mirror.

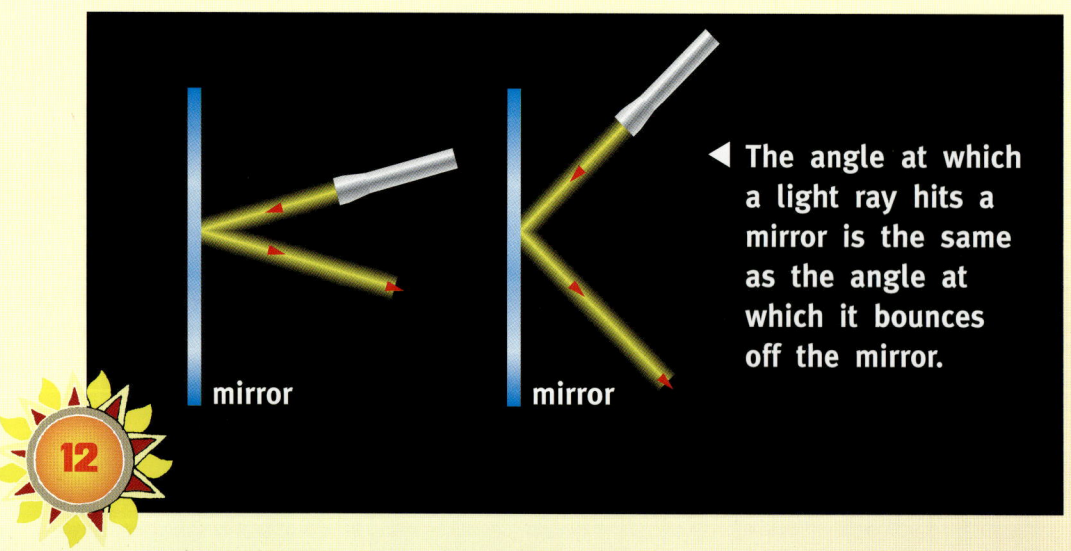

◀ **The angle at which a light ray hits a mirror is the same as the angle at which it bounces off the mirror.**

Your image is reversed, or backward. That is because light rays strike the mirror at an angle. The light rays bend and bounce off. The rays bounce in the other direction.

▲ The words on the book's cover are reversed.

Think of a ping-pong ball. The ball hits the table at a slant, or angle. Then the ball bounces off the table in the other direction. Light acts the same way.

Rough surfaces make light bounce differently. Look at your reflection in a puddle. The light reflects off of ripples. The light rays bounce every which way. The image gets jumbled.

▼ Light rays hitting the uneven surface of the puddle create a jumbled image.

CHAPTER 2

SPECIAL MIRRORS

Have you ever seen your reflection in a car door or bumper? You look smaller. The surface is **convex** (kahn-VEKS), or curved out. The convex surface shrinks your image. It also shows a wide view of the things behind you.

Car mirrors are convex. They let a driver see more of the road. They let a driver see other cars. That helps the driver judge the traffic.

Other mirrors are **concave** (kahn-KAYV). Concave mirrors curve in. They are hollowed out like a spoon. Concave mirrors are the opposite of convex mirrors.

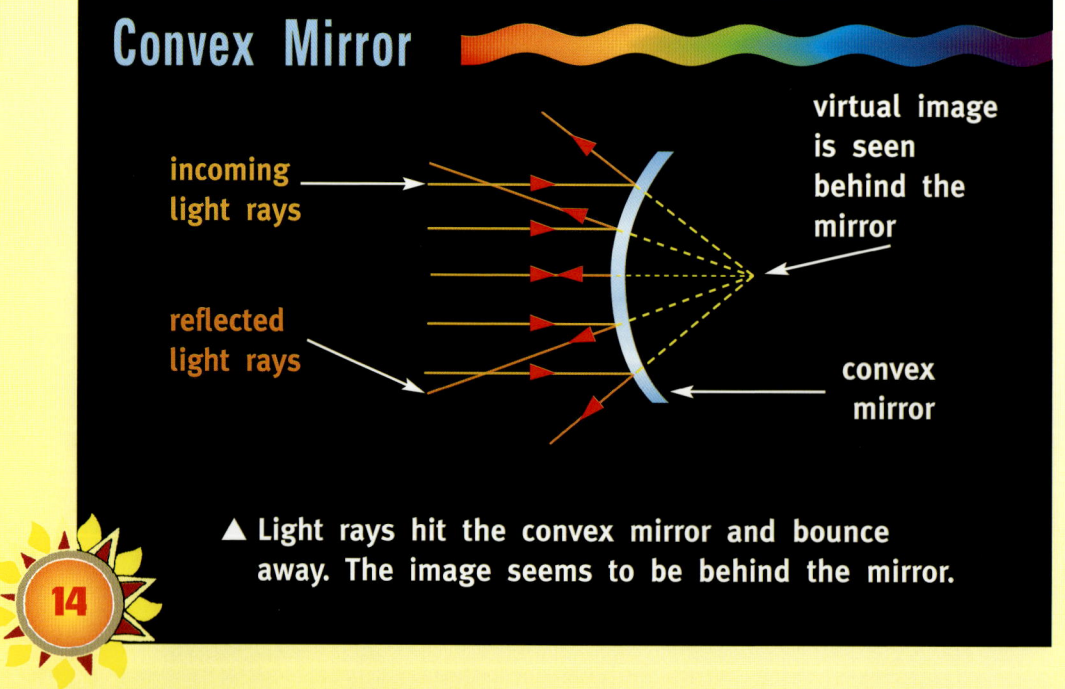

▲ Light rays hit the convex mirror and bounce away. The image seems to be behind the mirror.

MIRRORS AND LENSES

Look at yourself in a spoon. One side makes your head look big. That side is convex. The other side makes you look upside down. That side is the concave side.

Fun houses have mirrors. The mirrors change images. The mirrors have convex and concave surfaces. They make different parts of your body look larger or smaller.

▲ Fun houses use mirrors with concave and convex surfaces. The mirrors stretch and shrink parts of images.

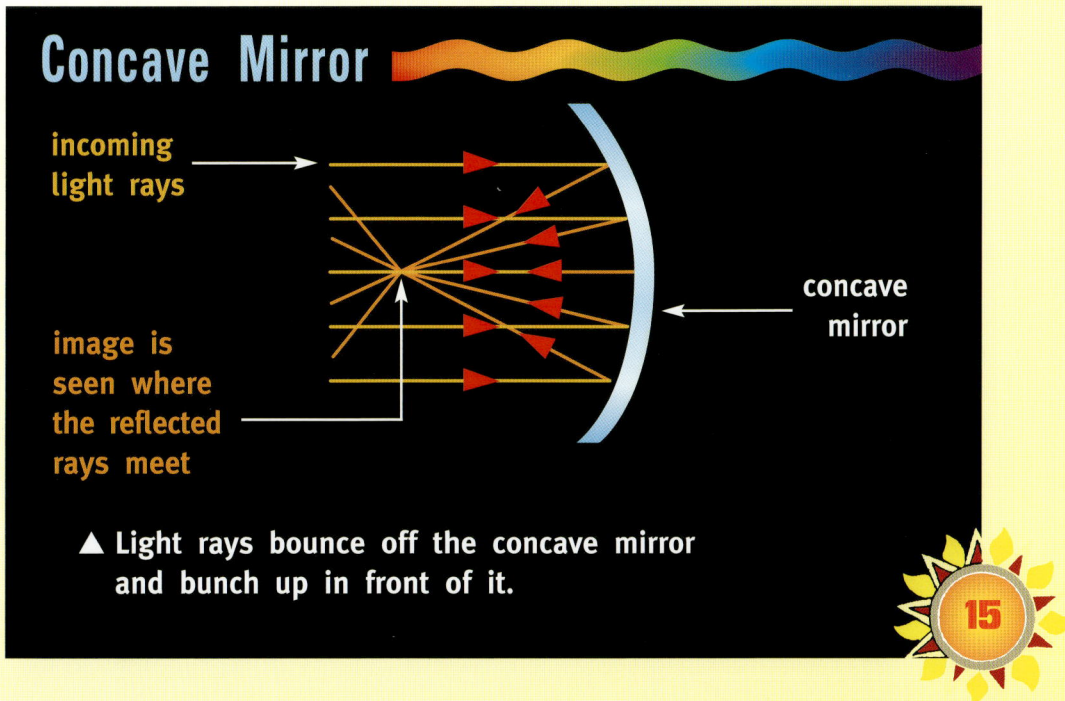

▲ Light rays bounce off the concave mirror and bunch up in front of it.

CHAPTER 2

LENSES

A lens is a piece of clear glass or plastic. Lenses have at least one curved surface. Lenses can be convex or concave. A lens makes things look bigger or smaller.

Some lenses are convex on both sides. These lenses make things seem bigger. Some lenses are concave on both sides. This type of lens makes things seem smaller.

▲ A lens that is convex on both sides makes things look bigger.

IT'S A FACT
The word "lens" comes from the Italian name for lentil beans. The beans are round like convex lenses.

convex   concave

MIRRORS AND LENSES

Some people cannot see things that are far away. These people wear glasses or contact lenses that are concave. Some people have trouble seeing things that are near. These people wear convex lenses.

▼ A magnifying glass enlarges objects.

CHAPTER 2

Lenses are stronger when we use them together. Telescopes have more than one lens. Telescopes let us see things that are very far away. They help us see stars and planets.

Some telescopes have two convex lenses. The front lens collects light from an object. The front lens reflects the light onto the second lens. The second lens is called the eyepiece. This lens magnifies the object. It makes the object bigger.

CAREERS IN SCIENCE

Optometrists fit people with eyeglasses and contact lenses that correct their vision. Optometrists work in private practices, clinics, or vision centers.

MIRRORS AND LENSES

A microscope is small. It has a few lenses. It has a front lens and an eyepiece lens. It also has a mirror. The mirror bounces light rays up. Then the light goes through a set of lenses. These lenses make tiny things big enough to see.

▲ A microscope has several lenses.

▲ A mirror and several lenses inside the microscope enlarge an object.

CHAPTER 3
COLOR, LIGHT, AND ENERGY

What color is light? Light looks white. It is really a mix of seven colors. The colors are red, orange, yellow, green, blue, indigo, and violet.

Why is the sky blue in the day? Why is the sky orange and red at sunset? The reason is that the air has tiny particles. These bits of gas and dust split the light into colors.

The sky looks blue because gas in the air scatters the blue rays. The blue rays reach our eyes. When the sun is low at sunset, the light looks orange and red. At sunset, those colors are scattered.

After a volcano erupts, the sunsets are very colorful. That is because the air has more dust. The added dust scatters more colors in the light.

RAINBOWS

Rainbows happen because of mist in the air. Mist is many tiny raindrops. Sometimes after a rain shower, the sun comes out. The sun shines light into the raindrops. The drops **disperse** (dih-SPERS), or split, the light. The white light is split into the colors of the rainbow.

▼ Rainbows appear after a shower, forming an arc of seven bands of color.

▲ Dust can make sunsets and sunrises more colorful.

21

CHAPTER 3

HANDS-ON EXPERIMENT
The Rainbow in a Glass of Water

- Fill a glass with water almost to the top.
- Place the glass near the edge of a table.
- Put a piece of white paper on the floor a few inches away from the table.
- Get a flashlight. Stick two pieces of solid tape (masking tape or electrical tape, not clear tape) over the front of the flashlight, leaving a thin slit about 1/8 inch (3 millimeters) wide.
- Turn on the flashlight and turn off the kitchen light.
- Shine the flashlight through both sides of the glass at an angle, aiming for the paper.

You will see a small rainbow on the paper. Do you think it matters whether you hold the flashlight so the slit is up and down, or across?

COLOR, LIGHT, AND ENERGY

You can make your own rainbow. Here is how it works. Try the experiment on page 22. The water and glass act like a **prism** (PRIH-zum). The water and glass bend and disperse the light. They split the white light into seven colors.

▼ A prism can be a clear block of glass. A prism splits light into a rainbow of colors. We call these seven colors the **visible spectrum** (VIH-zuh-bul SPEK-trum).

CHAPTER 3

They Made a Difference

The first ideas about light came from Sir Isaac Newton (below left). Newton was a scientist in the 1600s. He proved that light was not white. He found that it was made up of many colors.

Newton thought that light was the motion of tiny particles. Not all scientists agreed. In 1690, the scientist Christian Huygens (below right) said that light traveled in waves.

In 1704, Newton wrote a book called *Opticks*. It is one of the most important science books ever written.

Today we know that light is made of particles and waves. But in honor of Sir Isaac Newton and his famous book, we call the study of light *optics*.

COLOR, LIGHT, AND ENERGY

We see colors everywhere. Each color has a different wavelength. Some apples are red because they reflect light of the red wavelength. The apples absorb, or take in, the other wavelengths.

The yellow paint on a school bus absorbs all colors except for yellow. It sends only yellow light to your eyes.

▲ These apples are red because they absorb all the other colors.

CHAPTER 3

COLORS

Mix red and green paint. You will get brown paint. Mix red and green light. You will get yellow light. That is because when you mix light, you are adding wavelengths.

You can mix any two colors of light to make another. If you mix red and blue, you will get magenta (muh-JEN-tuh). If you mix blue and green, you will get cyan (SY-an). Mix red, green, and blue light. You will get white light. That is because their sum equals all the wavelengths of visible light.

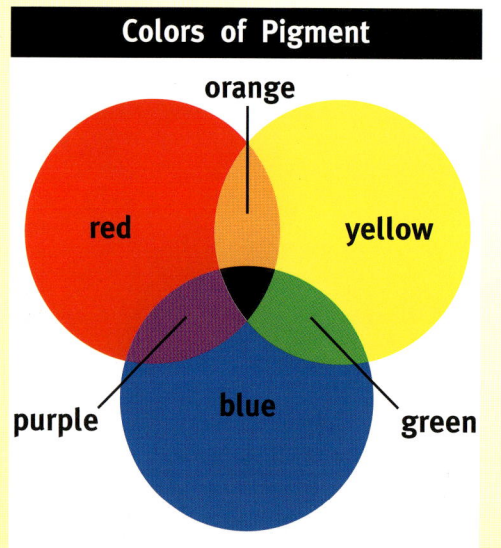
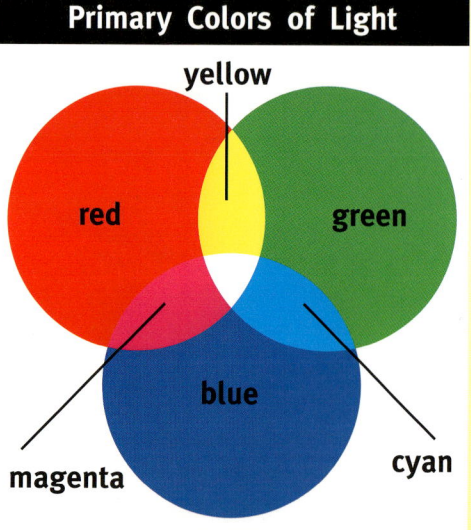

▲ The primary colors of pigment add up differently than the primary colors of light.

COLOR, LIGHT, AND ENERGY

They Made a Difference

In the late 1800s, artists in France used tiny dots of color. When you look at their paintings from far away, the dots cannot be seen. The dots blend into each other. The result is sometimes a brighter painting. If you look at the paintings up close, you can see the dots. This style of painting is called pointillism.

▲ This painting by Georges Seurat is called *Sunday in the Park on the Island of La Grande Jatte*. It contains about 3,456,000 dots of paint.

◀ Here you can see tiny dots of paint. They combine to make other colors when you stand far away.

CONCLUSION

Today we know a lot about light. We know what light is. We know how it works. We know that light moves in waves. We know that light can bend. We know that light has a spectrum of colors.

We need light to live. Light gives energy to all living things. Green plants grow because of sunlight. Light lets us grow food. Light gives color to the world around us. Light lets us see, read, and learn.

We use light in many ways. In recent years, we have found new ways to use light. Today, we use light to make energy. Solar panels collect light from the sun. The panels make the sun's light into heat. The panels make light into electricity, too. One solar station can make energy for thousands of homes!

✓ POINT

READ MORE ABOUT IT

What questions do you still have about light? Ask your teacher or librarian to help you find books and Internet sites where you can search for answers.

CONCLUSION

We can use the sun's light to run cars and buses. We even have solar airplanes.

We still have more to learn about light. We are always looking for new ways to use light. We are still thinking of ways to use solar power. How would you use solar power? Anything is possible!

▲ This plane is powered by solar energy.

GLOSSARY

concave (kahn-KAYV) a shape that is narrowest at the center and thicker at the edges (page 14)

convex (kahn-VEKS) a bulging shape that is wider in the center than at the edges (page 14)

crest (KREST) the highest part of a wave (page 7)

diffract (dih-FRAKT) to spread out under an object, as light does after hitting an edge (page 6)

disperse (dih-SPERS) to split light into the seven colors of a rainbow (page 21)

prism (PRIH-zum) a transparent, or clear, object that bends and splits light into colors (page 23)

reflect (rih-FLEKT) to bounce off at an equal angle (page 3)

refract (rih-FRAKT) to bend upon passing through a material (page 9)

trough (TROFF) the lowest part of a wave (page 7)

visible spectrum (VIH-zuh-bul SPEK-trum) the part of the electromagnetic spectrum that includes the colors we see (page 23)

wavelength (WAYV-lengkth) the distance between one crest and the next crest, or one trough and the next (page 7)

INDEX

absorb, 25

beams, 4

combine, 8, 27

concave, 14–17

convex, 14–18

crest, 7

diffract, 6, 8

disperse, 21, 23

energy, 4, 7, 28–30

interfere, 8

lens, 16–19

mirage, 11

primary colors, 26

prism, 23

reflect, 3, 12–15, 18, 25

refract, 9–10

trough, 7

visible spectrum, 23

wavelength, 7, 9, 25–26